GW00863808

101 Top Tips

On How to Grow Your Business

Through Referral

And

Word of Mouth Marketing

Welcome   6

Your Database   27

Segmenting Your Database   46

Knowing Your Numbers and Ratios   64

Building Your Relationship Plan   77

Committing to the Plan and Goal Setting   94

Summary   107

3

Copyright © 2013 Beach Group Publishing

All rights reserved. No part of this publication may be reproduced or transmitted in any form, or by any means, electronic, or mechanical, including photocopying, recording, or by any information storage or retrieval system.

Published by

Beach Group Publishing
153 Tilehouse Green Lane
Knowle
Solihull
B93 9EB

www.referralmaster.co.uk

ISBN: 978-1-291-26404-3

Retail Sales Rights granted to WWMD Ltd by the Copyright holder.

www.referralmaster.info

About the Author

Born in Watford in 1966, Barry Allaway has built up an extensive and impressive business portfolio during the course of his thirty-year career. With the last three decades spent in consumer magazine publishing sales and distribution, Barry has allocated his knowledge and expertise to a wide range of senior roles; most recently as Client Circulation and International Operations Director for IPC Media's Circulation arm (Marketforce). Barry's vast experience in referral marketing, alongside his renowned ability to significantly develop business growth, has made him a well known and reputable businessman in the UK.

Barry is married to Hazel, and has two teenage sons, Callum and Eachan. Outside of his working schedule, Barry enjoys sport, and is also a key component in the development of his sons' fossil and mineral business. He is also currently helping them undergo their own book publishing venture.

5

Acknowledgements

First and foremost, I would like to thank my immediate family, Hazel, Callum and Eachan, for putting up with many of my spare hours being dedicated to the creation of this book (even when watching Callum play rugby!). Thank you for your support, patience, and most of all, your constant belief in me.

I would also like to thank all of the people, without whom, this book wouldn't have been possible. To Steph Jones, Sarah Murray, Deepak and Sam, and Holly at Prontaprint - thank you for all you're design, print and editorial support. Also, thank you to my proofreaders, Steph Jones, Jacky Lawrence, Ashleigh Houfe and Hazel Allaway, and to Amer Amin, Sharn and Jim Franghiadi, John V Denley, Richard Markie and David Standing. Your assistance, guidance and honesty have helped to create something I am really proud of.

To all the Entrepreneur's Circle members, local BGAs and Inside Trackers (you know who you are) - thank you for your encouragement, support and feedback on the concepts I have shared with you.

Thank you to my parents, Carol and Alan Allaway, for always believing in me and providing me with the ambition and determination to turn my dreams into reality.

And finally, a big thank you to the late Jim Rohn, who's famous quote has enabled me to stick to my goals during the tough times ... "If the sky's the limit, how come there are footprints on the moon?"

Welcome

Congratulations on making such a wise purchase! By the small investment you've made in buying this book, you're already leaps ahead of the many competitors in your sector!

Written by Barry Allaway, the creator of the widely acclaimed Customer Pipeline for a Lifetime toolkit, this enjoyable and practical read provides detailed and informative tips on how to build and develop a successful business without the need for expensive 'throwing mud at the wall, and seeing what sticks' advertising.

Packed with invaluable advice and proven concepts from Barry himself along with many other industry experts, this book really is the 'must-have' read for anyone who is serious about becoming a super-successful business owner!

So now that you are on your way to running the kind of business you've always dreamt of, why stop here? All the helpful tips found in this book are expanded upon in the Customer Pipeline for a Lifetime toolkit, plus many more helpful resources, templates and support items.

All you will ever need to start raking in those profits and become a Referral Master can be found in the toolkit - there's a **special offer** on the toolkit for book purchasers at the back of the book so make sure you **grab a copy of the toolkit for yourself.**

Without further ado, let's get the ball rolling and put you on the right track to becoming a super-successful business owner!

Referral Master Tip # 1: No luck!

Have you ever called a millionaire 'lucky'? Have you ever looked at a yacht-owning, Ferrari-driving businessman and wondered why he seems to have all the 'luck' in the world?

Before you start to think that nothing like that could ever happen to you, let me firstly tell you that there is no such thing as luck when it comes to being successful. Of course, being in the right place at the right time can have a positive impact on your business (I would be a liar if I told you otherwise) but fundamentally; success is the result of hard work, determination and perseverance.

Believe it or not, those high-flying multimillionaires all had to start in the same place as you are. Each one of them had a dream; a vision of what they wanted out of life and every single one of them worked their socks off to make it come true.

Referral Master Nugget:

"Diligence is the mother of good luck."

Benjamin Franklin

Referral Master Tip # 2: Make decisions and take action...

Doing what you said you were going to do (or what you want to do) is a fundamental part of any successful business but it is even more important when it comes to building a business on referrals. To put it simply; how is anyone meant to refer you if they don't know who you are or what you do?

Making a decision is easy; putting it into action is what requires effort. People make decisions all the time; mostly everyone in the world has made the decision that they want to be wealthy and successful but only a very small percentage of people actually implement their plans. Remember that procrastination is a trait of the un-wealthy so don't put off until tomorrow what you can do today!

Referral Master Nugget:

No one ever got rich by just dreaming; they did so by taking the actions to make their dreams come true.

Referral Master Tip # 3: Be the optimist.

The only things that stand between you and your goals are the negative thoughts that keep you believing that you cannot achieve what you want to do.

In order to be super-successful, you cannot be a pessimist; you have to be an optimist. There are opportunities everywhere but only optimistic eyes will see them. That is the truth.

In order to truly believe that you *can* achieve your goals, you must get into the habit of looking for the positive in everything you do. Even when you are faced with rejections (which you will get), you have to keep going; and keep remembering why you are doing what you are doing. As human beings, we are all made of the same substances and all of us are given 24 hours a day and 7 days a week. In other words, every one of us has the potential to be whoever we want to be.

Referral Master Nugget:

"The Pessimist sees the difficulties in every opportunity - The Optimist sees the opportunity in every difficulty."

Jim Rohn

Referral Master Tip# 4: Work to live...

Many people think of work as a chore; a burden that gets in the way of what they really want to be doing. In order to be super-successful, you need to get out of this mindset. When you remove the graft, the stress and the pressure; work is simply something that determines the lifestyle you have.

Without work, and without earning a decent wage, you cannot live the life you desire or build the retirement pot you need for the future. Fact!

Think about how your lifestyle would be different if you didn't work hard. Would you still be living in the home that you are now? Would you still be driving the same car? Then, think about how much your lifestyle could further improve with a bit more of a push.

It is simple; the harder you work now, the more you can benefit in the future.

Referral Master Nugget:

"If you live well, you will earn well and you will attract like people and the circle starts all over again."

Jim Rohn

Referral Master Tip # 5: It's yourself you have to impress.

The Guy in the Glass

By Dale Wimbrow

When you get what you want in your struggle for pelf,

And the world makes you King for a day,

Then go to the mirror and look at yourself,

And see what the guy has to say.

For it isn't your Father, your Mother, or Wife,

Who judgement upon you must pass,

The feller whose verdict counts most in your life,

Is the guy staring back from the glass.

He's the feller to please, never mind all the rest,

For he's with you clear up till the end,

And you've passed your most dangerous, difficult test,

If the guy in the glass is your friend.

You be like Jack Horner and 'chisel' a plum,

And think you're a wonderful guy,

But the man in the glass says you're only a bum,

If you can't look him straight in the eye.

You can fool the whole world down the pathway of years,

And get pats on the back as you pass,

But your final reward will be heartache and tears,

If you've cheated the guy in the glass.

Referral Master Tip # 6: Be what you want to see...

Everyone has a dream about changing something in the world; we've all had those "If I was President..." conversations, yet most people believe that they are incapable of putting their dreams into action. How wrong they've got it!

If you've got a dream, then you've got a chance. Fact!

Super-successful people are the ones who believe 100% in their dreams and put them into action to make sure they come true. Super-successful people are the people who become the change that they want to see. If you want something, then you have to dream it, live it, see it, and *be* it. Think about it this way; if you wanted to be known as a non-smoker, then the first thing you would do is quite smoking! For the world to see your dream, you need to show it off.

Referral Master Nugget:

"Be the change you wish to see in the world."

Ghandi

Referral Master Tip # 7: Nigel Botterill advises - the best 90 minutes you'll ever spend!

You should spend 90 minutes a day doing something that will benefit your business. This 90 minutes should be spent when you are at your most productive (i.e. early morning), and during this time, you should find an area where you can work completely undisturbed. Yes, that's right, turn off your mobile (uh-oh), close your laptop and make yourself 'unavailable' to anyone else apart from yourself and your business.

This is a proven and widely-practised strategy that if stuck to everyday during the working week, will provide you with an extra 7.5 hours to get those jobs done that you 'haven't had the time to do.'

Maybe you need to fine-tune your sales letters, maybe you need to sort through application forms or maybe you need to finish sending out that list of invoices. Whatever it is that benefits your business, make sure you dedicate that daily 90-minute slot to get it done!

Referral Master Nugget:

Check out more from Nigel Botterill at www.e-c-guru.co.uk

Referral Master Tip # 8: Know the importance of professional relationships.

When building a business through referrals, the development of professional relationships is crucial to your success. Remember that people buy from people who they know, like and trust!

Here's a great example that demonstrates this:

Sarah is a freelance writer. She regularly writes web articles for a client who happens to be an internet marketing guru! Over a period of a few months, Sarah had built up a solid relationship with this client. He is always happy with her work and Sarah regularly makes an effort to communicate with him and keep in touch. So, when Sarah needs help advertising her services on the web, whom does she turn to for advice? Her internet marketing guru client, of course! Because Sarah is positively connected to this client, he is more than happy to assist and return the hard work that she puts in for him.

Referral Master Nugget:

The grass is greener at home more often than in someone else's field.

Referral Master Tip # 9: Use your people power!

You may be surprised to find out that despite living an era where copious amounts of communication is conducted via gadgets, people still prefer to deal with *people* over numbers, graphs and charts! Yes, that's right; believe it or not, most people (and by people I am of course referring to business owners as well as consumers) would much rather hear a friendly voice and see a smiling face in front of them, rather than simply being emailed the latest e-newsletter from your marketing team. Why? Because if people are going to part with their hard-earned cash, they want to know whose hands it's going into; they want to know that they can trust you to deliver what is being promised. Regardless of what the world may think, people favour doing business with a real person.

Referral Master Nugget:

How many people do you know who are not your typical 'geniuses' yet have made a success of themselves by 'being good' with people? Many, no doubt.

Referral Master Tip # 10: Be someone they remember.

A great reputation is a key factor in any successful business, and when it comes to building your business through referrals, it is one of the most important points.

First impressions go such a long way, so make sure you start as you mean to go on. I always recommend that as a business owner, you try to think from the perspective of the customer/referral partner.

What would you think if you were introduced to your business? Would you be left with a long-lasting impression or would your message merge with the thousands of others in your sector? What makes your business stand out?

The business world is a highly competitive industry so make sure your reputation always wins.

Referral Master Nugget:

It's all about them, and not about you...super-successful businesses do the hard things others won't do, to make the decision to do business with them easy for the other party.

Referral Master Tip # 11: Stay ahead.

When you think about all the contacts in your spheres of influence, which person quickly comes to mind? At the risk of sounding like a psychic mind-reader (which, by the way, I am certainly not), I can safely guess that it's the person you hear from most often; the person with whom you have a solid professional relationship and the person who makes that extra effort to do the things your other contacts do not do.

Maybe you haven't thought about it in this much detail before; maybe you haven't looked into the reasons why some people stand out more than others; but the reasons are there, and when you start to break it down, they are quite obvious.

Referral Master Nugget:

Your challenge is to make sure you and your business stand out from the crowd; you need to ensure your 'top of mind' and the 'go to' guy or girl that's known, trusted and liked by your key business contacts. Then you will pick up business that no-one else even hears about.

Referral Master Tip # 12: The chip shop...

Many years ago, I came to realise the huge importance of professional relationships. I remember the moment clearly; I was standing at a counter of a fish and chip bar when the owner stated that they had run out of vinegar. Instead of telling me I would have to go without, the owner picked up the phone and asked the person on the other end if he could borrow some vinegar until the manager returned from the suppliers. Within minutes, a man came through the door holding a box of vinegar sachets. I looked at the logo on his shirt and noticed that he was from the café across the road.

The strong and trusting relationship between these two business people was obvious. In a similar and competitive niche, they had created a solid connection where they were able to both depend and deliver. Both businesses are still going strong to this day.

Referral Master Nugget:

Instead of looking at other business owners as rivals, consider the ways in which you could help each other.

Referral Master Tip # 13: Don't be a one night stand.

A common mistake made by many business owners is to treat each customer or referral partner as a 'one night stand', getting from them what they need and then never contacting them again!

Think how often this has happened to you. Do you have a strong professional relationship with that guy you did business with three years ago? Has he kept in contact regularly and gone that extra mile to make you feel special? Is he the first contact you thought about when I asked you that question earlier? Probably not.

Most businesses are only concerned with their contacts when it suits them. Most businesses have to spend out large amounts of cash on advertising. You don't.

Building a successful business through referrals requires you to nurture long-lasting and durable professional relationships. Once you have mastered the art of this, you will have a lifetime of valuable referrals.

Referral Master Nugget:

Smart businesses make a sale to gain a long-term customer, not try and get a customer to make a sale.

Referral Master Tip # 14: Your window cleaner...

Imagine this situation; you have lived in the same property for a few years and ever since you moved in, the same window cleaner has been turning up regularly to clean your windows. (Keep reading, it will make sense soon, I promise.)This window cleaner always does a good job, and over the few years you have known him, you have built up a positive relationship. Every so often, promotional mail will get sent through your door advertising new window cleaners for very low prices. Even though these cleaners are claiming to be cheaper that anyone else around (including your regular guy) and promise a regular and reliable service, you ignore their brilliant offers. Why? Because you know, like and trust the existing cleaner you have. You have built up a relationship with your existing window cleaner and you would rather give your money to him over any new company, regardless of how good/cheap they claim to be.

Referral Master Nugget:

"The best way to find out if you can trust somebody is to trust them."

Ernest Hemmingway

Referral Master Tip # 15: A network of opportunity!

How many members of your family or friends eat in the same restaurants, drink at the same bars and shop at the same supermarkets? The point is that somewhere down the line, referrals have influenced your decision-making process without you realising. Have you read a good book lately or seen a great film? Maybe you've received excellent service at a local bar or restaurant, or been on holiday to a great hotel. Whatever positive experience you've had, I am sure you have told others about it.

It has to be worked at, but I try 110% to ensure everyone in my networking sphere is of some benefit to my business (and mine to them) either through using or purchasing each other's products and services, or at the very least, ensuring I know what they do and how they can help others I meet to make referrals and recommendations.

Referral Master Nugget:

Good referrals make a massive positive impact on your business sales funnel, and finding out how to create a steady supply of them is important if you want to be super-successful.

Referral Master Tip # 16: People are sick of the boring, same old sales techniques!

These days, everyone seems to know how to knock out a decent sales letter or how to use cheesy 'objection handling techniques'. The sheer extent of call centres and door-to-door salesmen has enabled most people to be able to spot a sales pitch a mile off. By building your business through referral marketing, you are immediately setting yourself apart from the majority of businesses out there, and you are giving your contacts/referral partners the chance to get to know *you*; not just your previous, 'same as the rest' sales hype.

Ultimately, when conducting business, people want honesty. And who can blame them? Why should anyone be expected to part with their hard-earned cash on the basis of a generic old school sales pitch?

Referral Master Nugget:

Using a referral plan effectively will cut out 70% of the traditional sales cycle, and in turn; increase conversion rates and significantly reduce the time it takes from first contact to sale.

Referral Master Tip # 17: Be yourself.

If you want to be able to create long-lasting, professional relationships, it's important that you stay true to who you are.

Of course, you wouldn't talk to your business contacts in the same way that you would speak to your friends at the pub (well not all of them anyway) but you should still be yourself - just the best version of it.

Look at the list of qualities below and decide which **three** suit your personality best:

I am friendly □

I always do what I say I am going to do □

I am a good timekeeper □

I am trustworthy □

I am confident □

Referral Master Nugget:

Remember, it's not about trying to be the perfect person; it's about recognising your best qualities and always conveying them to your contacts.

Referral Master Tip # 18: Forget about the corporate BS!

Behind the business suits, shirts, polished shoes, boardrooms and corporate commercialism, people want to be able to know, like and trust the people they are dealing with. Everyone knows that personal ethos and reputation make a massive difference to how others see you, yet in business, people seem to retract themselves from this theory.

I'll admit, statistics and selling techniques can be impressive, but being referred through a reputable mutual acquaintance is 110% better than cold calling, even if the cold caller claims he has just fitted out David Beckham's new kitchen!

Referral Master Nugget:

What would you be more inclined to believe - the sales pitch of a travel agent telling you about the 'magnificence' of certain destination or the opinion of a friend who has actually been there?

Your Database

Referral Master Tip # 19: Get a new best friend.

Who is your best friend? You know - the person you can rely on for anything; the one you trust with your life. Is it the oldest friend in your phonebook? Is it the person you met at a party and instantly 'clicked' with? Well it shouldn't be. As a business owner, your very best friend should always be your database!

Don't worry; I haven't gone crazy and I am not about to tell you to start talking to your database about your deepest secrets (because that *would* be crazy) but what I am saying is that you should treat your database with care and attention, because as your best friend, it will give to you *what you give* to it. If you nurture your database, communicate with it thoroughly, and give it the information it needs to function, then you will prosper in the rewards; it's simple.

Referral Master Nugget:

"Your database will be your business's greatest asset when you develop it and implement from it effectively."

Nigel Botterill, CEO and Founder, *Entrepreneur's Circle* (Nigel has created an offer for you at www.e-c-guru.co.uk).

Referral Master Tip # 20: Say sorry!

When beginning to build a strong and fully -functional database, the very first communication you make is to apologise to all your existing contacts (no matter how long you haven't been in touch with them) for previously being so poor in your past communication. Advise them that you are seeking to be a better communicator and that from now on, they can expect to hear from you regularly. I know, I know; no one likes to swallow their pride and most of the time, sorry does seem to be the hardest word. But, being honest with your clients will automatically earn you their respect and you will probably be surprised to discover that they will be happy to hear from you.

Referral Master Nugget:

If you are uncomfortable laying out a formal apology, maybe consider incorporating a touch of humour in your approach. For example:

"Hi Joe, Sorry I haven't been in touch for a while, but I am now back on the scene and will be in touch a lot more often. Don't panic; I am not going to bombard you with sales pitches (not bad ones anyway)..."

Referral Master Tip # 21: There's a place for everyone.

These days, people seem to 'know' more people than ever. Whether it is Facebook 'friends', Twitter followers or LinkedIn connections, there has never been a time where people have been in better contact with the world. So, when you are starting to build a successful business, you should find these contacts a place in your database. Remember that you are in contact with these people for a reason; so think about the ways in which they could become valuable assets to your success. If you are a hairdresser, for instance, then look at all of your connections within this sector. There may be people, such as suppliers or past customers, who you don't have much contact with, but find them a place anyway!

Referral Master Nugget:

Remember it is not just who you know, it's who your contacts know that matters.

Referral Master Tip # 22: Start thinking about F.R.O.G.S.

No; I am not talking about small, slithery animals that go 'ribbit', I am talking about your Friends, Relations, Organisations, Groups and Social. (F.R.O.G.S.)

In order to fill your all-important database with as many valuable contacts as possible, you should always think outside the box. Maybe you are part of a sports team or a member of a club. Think about all the people with whom you share a common interest and find them a place in your database!

It's a good idea to start to think of your database as a virtual people network and try to extend your network chain as broadly as possible.

Referral Master Nugget:

F.R.O.G.S. will give your database the 'leap' to being multi-layered and multi-functional and will be a massive resource and future asset in your businesses success.

Referral Master Tip # 23: It's not who you know, it's who they know that matters!

You may be surprised to discover this, but most people know around 250 people who they know well enough that they can strike up a conversation with. So, if you know 250 people, and each of those 250 contacts know another 250 people, that is 62,500 people who you could do business with through an active referral network!

If you try to add at least five contacts to your database every day, you'll soon be on your way to building a substantial network of valuable contacts.

Referral Master Nugget:

If you can't think of 250 people off the top of your head, look through your old phone books, address books, Christmas card lists, Friends Reunited, Facebook, LinkedIn and other social media contacts. You will be pleasantly surprised at how quickly you can develop your list and with 62,500 contacts from your first level contacts; that should be more than enough to keep you busy and your business growing.

Referral Master Tip # 24: Out of your mind and into an action!

Creating a large and functional database may leave you feeling daunted, so jot down all your thoughts and ideas on a piece of paper. Write down the names of contacts you know (even if you're unsure if they are relevant) and start to think about how these people can benefit your business.

Map out ways in which you can find new contacts and refer to your 'mind map' every time you feel the pressure!

Brainstorming is an excellent way of organising your thoughts and ideas and can really help to make you feel more focused in your plans.

Referral Master Nugget:

"Vision without action is merely a dream. Action without vision just passes the time. Vision with action can change the world!"

Joel Arthur Barker

Referral Master Tip # 25: Make the most of the internet.

If you currently use Facebook, LinkedIn (we'll speak more about this later) or any other social networking site, I would advise you to take a good look at your contacts' working sector and think about whether they (or more importantly, their contacts) could be advantageous to your business.

You may not have thought about it like this before, but your social sphere can potentially hold massive benefits to your success. Maybe you have Facebook friends who are in similar sectors to you; but because you class them as social acquaintances, you haven't previously recognised this connection. Think about the chain of referrals these contacts could bring.

Referral Master Nugget:

"Relationships are all there is. Everything in the universe only exists because it is in relation to everything else. Nothing exists in isolation. We have to stop pretending that we are individuals who can go it alone."

Margaret Wheatley

Referral Master Tip # 26: Visualise your future.

Many people make the mistake of allowing the effort of planning to overrun their dreams for the future. Instead of seeing planning as a chore, try to enjoy it. Visualise the end result and think of planning as a stepping stone to get there.

When creating your database, try to look at every contact as a potential customer/ referral partner. If any of your contacts are a drain on you, then do the brave thing and jettison them! Remember that a database is only powerful if it is nurtured and developed and you simply can't afford to keep the 'naysayers' and miserable old gits who keep dragging you down on your way to being super-successful!

Although there is certainly potential in numbers, a large database alone will not place you on the road to super-success; it needs to be functional!

Referral Master Nugget:

Instead of thinking of each contact as an addition to your database, think about what qualities they could bring to helping your dreams come true, whilst also benefiting your contacts!

Referral Master Tip # 27: SPECIAL GUEST TIP:

Build a people network.

Name: Amer Amin

Company: Find Me Local (UK) Ltd

Website: www.FindMeLocal.co.uk

"When attending a networking event, I always go in with a goal in mind. It is amazing how a filter sets in and your mind starts filtering observations and events with an emphasis toward achieving the goal. But the most important is not to just seek to get, but always to find ways to give something to others you meet. It does not have to be a major thing. Sometimes just a small effort of helping someone with a contact or with an idea can be big help for the others. So always seek to give. I always make a few notes on their business card about what I could give to them. And I act on it as quickly as I can while the relationship with the new person is fresh. Your act of giving makes the fresh relationship become a bit deeper very quickly.

The interesting thing is that the more I give, the more I also get back."

Referral Master Tip # 28: Keep focused and target effectively.

Many people fail to build a usable database simply because they don't include relevant contacts. It may sound obvious and you are probably thinking that no one in their right mind would build up a database of irrelevant contacts; but it happens; and all too regularly!

Use the small checklist below to identify a quality contact:

- Is the contact within/linked to my sector? □
- Can my product /service benefit the contact? □
- Is the contact likely to have a substantial contact network that will benefit my business and help my own contacts? □

Referral Master Nugget:

This checklist is just a guideline, and there will always be exceptions to the rules; but try to get into the habit of asking yourself these questions before you fall into the trap of building a stagnant database.

Referral Master Tip # 29: Stop, look, listen!

Every business owner dreams of super-success, but unfortunately, most do not make it. Putting aside the many reasons why this is so, there is a common denominator that merges the unsuccessful; failure to listen!

Some business owners have a vision so strong that they are not prepared to listen to the expert advice of others who know the industry or market place better.

Even the most prosperous of business owners need advice; no one makes it based on their own knowledge alone. Does David Beckham base his enormous success just on his soccer skills? Of course not! Throughout his career (and still to this day), he has had to listen to the advice of experts around him, no doubt having to adjust his plans from time to time.

Remember that pride is a lot easier to swallow than failure, so don't get caught up in what you *think* is right.

Referral Master Nugget:

"It takes a great man to give sound advice tactfully, but it takes a greater to accept it graciously."

Logan P. Smith

Referral Master Tip # 30: Merge your urge!

Before reading these hints and tips, it's quite likely that you had a few separate lists of contacts. Now is the time to merge them together.

Set a few hours aside to put all of your contacts into one list. With segmentation, your full database will be immensely powerful and you will have everything you need right in front of you and you will feel a lot more organised and in control. Once you start merging your lists, you will, no doubt, come across some contacts that you forgot you even had that you can re-engage with-you never know what they have been up to recently and how you may be of benefit to each other.

Seek to find a Cloud solution for your database, or at the very least, save the files on-line so you can access them anywhere, add to them and enhance your contact knowledge base at any time.

Referral Master Nugget:

If you are not using a Cloud-based Customer Relationship Management system, then a simple Excel file in a drop box folder (www.dropbox.com) is an easy place to start.

Referral Master Tip # 31: Get a system.

In time, I would recommend that you get a decent Customer Relationship Management (CRM) system, but for now, any scalable database system will do just fine.

The important thing to consider is if you are confident in using the system, and if it does the job you want it to do! Microsoft Excel is a perfectly acceptable starting place and something that is easy to learn how to use, and even more importantly, easy to export data into and out of when the time comes for you to migrate onto a more sophisticated system in the future.

Referral Master Nugget:

If you feel daunted and overwhelmed by the thought of creating a database system, why not employ a virtual assistant (VA)? You never know, if they do a great job on your database system, then you could hire them for other jobs in the future!

Can't find a VA? Ashleigh Houfe of First Class VA (www.firstclassva.co.uk) is our first port of call for admin support.

Referral Master Tip # 32: Separate your fields.

It is important that you have each element of your data in a separate field as it will make your database so much more powerful later on. As simple as it may sound, many people I help with database advice make the simple error of not separating out contacts and surnames in their data. If you have a contact called John Smith, for example, you must create one entry for 'John' and one entry for 'Smith'. The reason for this is that when you come to search for this client, you can search by 'John' or 'Smith'. Additionally, when you come to send communications to the customer, you can build documentation and letters with the segmented names woven into the body of the letter.

Referral Master Nugget:

"It makes sense to invest in new work. It's almost like having a research department in a scientific laboratory. You have to try things out. You'll make some bad mistakes. Some things will fail but at least you'll energise the organisation."

Gavin Bryars

Referral Master Tip # 33: Shape up!

Once you have your database system in place, it's time to think about its structure.

Here's a simple and effective template to get you started:

(First name) John
(Surname/Second name) Smith
(Date of Birth) 14/01/1962
(Address) 1 The High Street
(County / District) i.e. Devon or Arizona
(Country) United Kingdom / USA
(Postcode / Zip Code
(Partner's name) i.e. Claire
(Mobile phone) 44 9999 9999
(Where we met) i.e. Chamber of Commerce/Trade

Referral Master Nugget:

Don't forget to add:

a) Notes section to add basic contact / other data and personal information;
b) Industry specific section – where you can add specific information to your business /sector i.e. waist size of customer for a tailor.

Referral Master Tip # 34: There's no such thing as too much information!

You may be wondering why trivial information such as partner's names and dates of birth are important. Before now, your database (if you had one) was likely to have consisted of simply a name, a telephone number and an email address.

Being aware of basic personal information can really set you apart from your competitors. Knowing a client's partner's name, for example, means you can send more personalised Christmas cards and knowing a client's date of birth allows you to send small 'keep in touch' gifts at appropriate times. It can also lay strong foundations for promotional marketing. Showing a client that you have 'done your homework' and put in the effort to maintain your professional relationships will automatically propel your reputation.

Referral Master Nugget:

"Continuous effort - not strength or intelligence - is the key to unlocking our potential."

Winston Churchill

Referral Master Tip # 35: Minor actions can make a big difference!

In business, it's important to remember that your small plans are as significant as your large ones. Many people allow their visions of the end result to overshadow the minor actions that they must apply in other to turn the dream into reality.

So, whereas you may think that correctly structuring your database can wait until next week; it can't. However inconsequential or tedious a small task may appear, you must get into the habit of understanding how the actions you implement today can have a vital influence on the future of your business.

The small actions you take at the start will have substantial consequences. I always say that it's easier to work this way from the start, than having to pay a lot of money on a temp, or spending a lot of time yourself putting it right later on.

Referral Master Nugget:

Why not hire a virtual administrative assistant to help you out? Ashleigh Houfe of www.firstclassva.co.uk does a great job for us or you can find all sorts of outsourced support via Elance at www.elance.com

Referral Master Tip # 36: SPECIAL GUEST TIP:

It really does work!

Name: Sharn and Jim Franghiadi

Company: JSF Driver **Training Ltd and JSF Driving School**

Web: http://jsfdrivingschool.co.uk/

"As a business, we have always recorded customer contact details and outcomes on paper; generating stats and tracking our marketing with that information. Then someone mentioned a database system! In preparation for a database installation, we moved most of that information on to Excel spreadsheets and placed it in useful categories tailored to our businesses needs. Now we are looking forward to the improved communication and personal relationship building that our database will allow, generating more sales and reviews as we also get to grips with the new CRM. Targeted, planned communication will make the selling easier, letting us 'touch' customers in a more systemised manner... and grow money for our business!"

Segmenting Your Database

Referral Master Tip # 37: Give to get!

Unsuccessful business owners make the crucial mistake of thinking they can get something for nothing. Because they run a business, have worked hard in setting it up and spend money on advertising, most business owners expect to start reaping in the rewards straight away. The real world no longer works like this.

Think about the friendships you have in your life; these friendships were not formed overnight and I can guarantee that if you asked your best friend for a favour on the first day that you met, you would have been met with a different response to what you get today! All relationships (be them professional or personal) must work on a two-way street; they must be mutually beneficial for both parties involved. In other words, you can't expect to get anything without giving something first.

Referral Master Nugget:

"The real rule of give and take is.... before you can take you gotta give."

Jeffrey Gitomer

Referral Master Tip # 38: Use the power of four.

Segmenting your database will allow you to effectively target your contacts and give you an enormous head start over others within your sector.

I recommend that you split your database into four segments:

VIRPs - c20 Very important referral partners

Golds - The next 20-30 influential contacts

Silvers - The contacts you are in the process of building a relationship with

Developing - The contacts you hope to develop a relationship with.

Remember that the level of communication that you have with your contacts from each category will differ, so be diligent during the selection process.

Referral Master Nugget:

Don't panic if you can't decide which segment a contact should go into; go with your gut feeling first...you can always move them into a different segment at a later date.

www.referralmaster.info

Referral Master Tip # 39: Dedicate yourself to your database.

As you start to think of your different groups of contacts, I would recommend that you dedicate a weekly or fortnightly 60-minute slot in your diary to continue to fine-tune your segments.

Mastering the act of segmenting your database is not something that will come overnight. Depending on the amount of contacts you have in your database (which is hopefully a number that is constantly growing); it is unrealistic to expect to be able to do this quickly. This is a practice that requires focus and thought and so doing it on a weekly/fortnightly basis will give you the time you need to get to grips with things.

Referral Master Nugget:

Your Very Important Referral Partners (VIRPs) list is where only your most valuable relationships reside, so try to keep its membership below 20 initially, and no more than 50 at any one time to keep it special for them, and a manageable focus and investment in time and expenditure for you.

Referral Master Tip # 40: LinkedIn!

If you do not use LinkedIn, start using it today! Even if social networking is something you swore you would never do, allow LinkedIn to be the reason you break your rule. I will tell you why.

For those of you who are unfamiliar with LinkedIn, it is fundamentally an online business community (similar to Facebook or Friends Reunited without the embarrassing holiday poolside pictures) completely focused on generating more business growth and opportunities. Currently, on LinkedIn, I have over 2,900 first level contacts. Through those contacts, on my second level within LinkedIn, I have over 1,500,000 potential contacts and on my third level (where I can mine for help, guidance and potential future business partnerships), I have a staggering 22,032,857 potential future business partners in my LinkedIn sphere with whom I can seek a relationship through my first and second level contacts.

Referral Master Nugget:

Whilst not as powerful as your own database, LinkedIn is a great tool to utilise when searching for new contacts and opportunities, for your database and business development plan.

Referral Master Tip # 41: Invest the right time and effort in your database segments.

Segmenting your database is all about providing you with better opportunities to nurture your relationships. In other words, there is absolutely no point in creating these segmentations if you are going to ignore their purpose.

When you are creating your crucial Keep in Touch plan, you should always invest more time, money and effort into your VIRPs than any other segment in your database. Bear in mind, however, that each contact in your database has the potential to become a VIRP in the future and so their importance should not be overlooked.

Referral Master Nugget:

The Customer Pipeline for a Lifetime toolkit contains highly detailed and invaluable advice on nurturing your relationships with your segmented contacts. There's an exclusive offer at the back of the book to enable you to get your own copy of the toolkit at a special 'Referral Master book readers' price.

Referral Master Tip # 42: There are mines of diamonds right under your feet!

Many businesses fall into the trap of spending vast sums of money and effort focusing on winning new customers and/or clients to the detriment of the clients and customers they already have.

As experts in the field, we know that it takes five times as much effort and cost to find a new customer as it does to keep a current customer happy and buying from you.

We're not saying not to prospect for new customers (that's what referrals are all about) but we *are* saying that you should never neglect what you already have. The grass is usually not greener on the other side of the fence and spending some time and effort engaging with your current customers is the smart way to maximise your businesses potential

Referral Master Nugget:

Invest in a good printed and mailed newsletter (yes, printed and mailed newsletters are rare these days but *do* get read whereas email PDF newsletters get treated as spam and deleted). www.newsletterguy.co.uk can help if needed.

Referral Master Tip # 43: There is no sales slowdown that can't be solved by a great sales letter.

The only thing that sits between a great product/service and a sale are the right words written/spoken in the correct way.

Many people seem to dismiss the importance of great content (or 'copy' as it is known in the industry), but the fact remains if you get your words right, your customers will be putty in your hands!

Creating excellent copy is especially important when keeping in touch with each segment of your database (your written content will be representing you and your company; so you need to get it spot on!)

Referral Master Nugget:

If you find yourself suffering from 'writer's block' or you just cannot think of a way to demonstrate on paper just how amazing your company is, we recommend Stephanie Jones of Say It Write. You can contact Steph via e-mail at: steph@wesayitwrite.com

Referral Master Tip # 44: Smile and the world will smile with you!

It's crucial that when you are keeping in touch with your database contacts, you always communicate in a positive and happy manner - even if you have had a bad day!

Remember that your reputation goes a long way towards the success of your business and you want to make sure that you are thought about in a positive way. It's all well and good keeping in regular contact, but it's how you convey yourself that *really* matters. To be a super-successful business person, you need to be able to put on a great performance, even if your car has just broken down, your latest contract proposal has been rejected or your you are just having 'one of those days'!

You must never let your negative emotions get in the way of positive communication.

Referral Master Nugget:

"Negative people are worse than negative occurrences. An argument is over in ten minutes - the person may hang around for years."

Jeffrey Gitomer

Referral Master Tip # 45: No one is going to come knocking at your door!

If you want to be successful in business, you have got to accept the fact that when you start out, *you* have to make contact with people. If you sit around waiting for the 'next big customer' to come knocking at your office door, you are going to be waiting for a very long time!

In order to prove that you care about your contacts and in order to ensure that you stay at the top of their minds, you have to put in the time, work and effort. Remember that most business owners will not be doing this, so make sure you give yourself that head start over your competitors!

Referral Master Nugget:

Remember to be patient! In business today it is taking up to seven contacts/'touch points' before a business makes a decision on purchasing, so don't expect overnight results. A super-successful business requires perseverance, persistence and consistency. If you fall at the first hurdle, keep going as most business owners give up too early and lose out on the business opportunity because of this.

Referral Master Tip # 46: Make them feel special...

In order to make sure you and your business stands out from the crowd, and in order to keep your company at the forefront of your contacts' minds, you must go that extra mile; and do the things that other business owners are not prepared to do, to make customers feel special.

When thinking of ways to do this, it's a good idea to look back at the information you included into your database fields at the beginning (you see, it all ties together in the end!) Think about the specific areas your contacts are interested in (sport, fashion, reading, etc) and think of ways you can incorporate gifts, events or entertainment around them.

Small gestures make big impacts and go a long way in showing your contacts that you care.

Referral Master Nugget:

If you are sending gifts to your contacts, then why not get them branded with your company details for further exposure? Remember to keep it subtle – the main focus should be on the contact and not you.

Referral Master Tip # 47: Questions are the answers...

It's a fact; people like to talk about themselves-especially business owners!

When liaising with a contact, it's a good idea to remember that you have two ears and one mouth and to use them in proportion. Speaking and listening on a 2:1 ratio will show the contact that you are interested in what they have to say and will immediately start to develop their trust in you. Similarly, your questions should be left 'open' so that the contact has the chance to be receptive. The more information the contact discloses, the more chance there is for you to provide an opportunity for business.

Referral Master Nugget:

I would highly recommend that you get your hands on a copy of *'Questions are the Answers'*, by Allan Pease.

You will also find an abundance of practical advice on the Customer Pipeline for a Lifetime Facebook page – www.facebook.com/referralmaster

Referral Master Tip # 48: Never give up...communicating!

These days, with the heaps of 'communication and noise' that people get on a daily basis, it is taking longer and longer for contacts to absorb the information we give to them.

Back in the 70s and 80s, buying decisions were usually made after just 3 or 4 communications, but in this modern age, (where people are more accessible to receive more information, it is taking far longer). Through a lack of patience, perseverance and understanding of the industry, most businesses give up after a few contact attempts. Smart businesses, on the other hand, keep going; eventually making a sale.

Being a successful business owner requires you to be a marathon runner; not a sprinter, and endurance wins over speed every time.

Referral Master Nugget:

When do you take a contact off your prospect list? When they become a customer (or opt out or die!).

Referral Master Tip # 49: The easy way to get more referrals....

It always amazes me how many people fail to ask satisfied clients and customers for referrals! If you don't do this, you are leaving massive business opportunities untapped.

The best time to ask for a referral is after you have delivered your product and service and you know that the customer or client is happy,

Build a 'referral request plan' into your business sales funnel and see how it will make a positive impact on your business.

Referral Master Nugget:

Ask every satisfied customer or client for three people who they know, who could also benefit from your product or service and then add them to your sales funnel and follow up...follow up...follow up!

Referral Master Tip # 50: Brand it up!

Subtly branded gifts are a fantastic way to show your contacts that you care and give your company some further exposure at the same time.

Stationery items such as pens and notepads are especially useful for branding as your contacts will use these on a regular basis.

It is inexpensive and easy to get gifts branded and it will immediately demonstrate to the contact that you are prepared to go that extra mile for them.

The important thing to remember about branding is to keep it subtle.

Referral Master Nugget:

Find yourself an innovative and creative sales promotions partner who can help manage this for you...the better their ideas, the more business you will generate and hence the more you can invest in the process next time around...so its win/win when you get the right partner on board. Steve Cooke is our go to guy – www.cre8tivebrandideas.co.uk

Referral Master Tip # 51: How much, how often?

We all know those people (be they friends, relatives or professional acquaintances) who only ever get in touch when they need something, and let's face it, it is quite annoying and not a great feeling!

In order to build and develop strong and withstanding professional relationships, you need to provide a steady flow of communication. Obviously, too much contact can be just as detrimental as none at all; so you need to ensure that you get the balance just right.

It's a good idea to devise a communication structure for each of your database segments and start implementing it straight away. Once you have a structure in place, your contacts will expect to hear from you on a daily/ weekly/ monthly basis and will feel quite disappointed if you fail to stay in touch.

Referral Master Nugget:

By executing a systemised communication plan, you will create a sense of trust and security with your contacts, and you will remain at the top of their minds.

Referral Master Tip # 52: SPECIAL GUEST TIP:

How to make GroupOn actually work for you...

Name: John V Denley

Company: DiaryBooker.com Ltd

Website: www.DiaryBooker.com

Maybe you have wondered if something like GroupOn is something that you might like to use, but have heard stories about how businesses that do use them get a sudden rush of customers, but then they never come back again for a second appointment. Most customers don't go back because they have simply forgotten about the business they went to. What you need is to give them a reminder about their experience and a reason to come back.

What almost all of these businesses are not doing is capturing the information about who is coming in, when they came in, what services they used and then using this information to encourage them to come back again and again, by marketing back to them. This is a big mistake and this is where you can really help to make those customers stick around and keep coming back to you for years, especially if you have a system, which will automatically do all this remarketing for you.

Referral Master Tip # 53: Moving Up Into the Next Category...

As you develop and nurture your relationships with your segmented contacts, there will come a time when you feel they deserve a place in a higher category, for example, when they start passing you more referrals, or alternatively, if they don't treat a referral you give them as well as you expect, you may move them from your key group (VIRPs) down a level or two. The decision to move a contact up a tier is a subjective one and can only be made by you. It's a good idea to work out an 'entry requirement list' for each category to ensure that the contacts justify moving up a place in your database.

Referral Master Nugget:

Create a weekly/fortnightly database diary slot dedicated to fine-tuning your database and the segmentation within it to maximise its power. Think of it as a weekly tune-up of your car's engine to get maximum performance.

Knowing Your Numbers and Ratios

Referral Master Tip # 54: Is it a job or a hobby?

Most business owners are doing something they enjoy and, while that is something that is envied amongst many of the employed, it does come with the danger of seeming like a hobby instead of a job.

When you work for yourself, it is easy to become 'scrappy' when it comes to your numbers and figures. During slow periods, it may be tempting to 'do a deal' or lower your asking price for the chance of getting a sale, and although this is sometimes necessary, you must be able to justify your actions.

Being a good business owner means being aware of your numbers and ratios at all times. No matter how much you love your job, its number one purpose is to make you money - not to become an expensive hobby!

Referral Master Nugget:

Super-successful businesses have found ways and developed systems/processes that enable them to earn money whilst they sleep...now that's a nice feeling when you go to bed!

Referral Master Tip # 55: Know the importance of knowing your numbers.

If you know your numbers and ratios, you know what works and what doesn't work for your company's profitability. In turn, you can then continue doing what works and change and improve on what doesn't work (operationally as well as on the sales and marketing front). The concept is really that simple.

If you worked for a company, you would expect the directors and managers to know exactly how the company is performing. As a business owner, you need to develop the same discipline for yourself, and a whole lot more. You will never be taken seriously as a business owner unless you start thinking seriously about your numbers and ratios. Furthermore, how can you expect to make serious money if you don't take your business seriously?

Referral Master Nugget:

If you are struggling to get your head around your figures, why not ask your accountant for advice? If they can't help then you need a new accountant.

Referral Master Tip # 56: Successful business owners are all psychic (or are they just clever?)

If you were asked how much you expected to earn this year, would you know the answer? Maybe you have a hopeful figure in your mind but haven't a clue how you're going to achieve it.

So, how exactly do you plan your profits without having the ability to see into the future?

First of all, decide on how much profit you want to make this year. Then, figure out how much money and time you need to spend on marketing/investment. It's not about 'waiting to see how much you make', it's about *deciding* how much you are going to make, and building a plan and implementing it to ensure you achieve it as a minimum.

The fact is successful business owners are not psychic; they simply place the future in their own hands.

Referral Master Nugget:

Once you know your numbers, you will be able to calculate the lifetime value of a client or customer...then you will know how much you can afford to spend to find more of them, and what you can afford to invest to keep the ones you already have.

Referral Master Tip # 57: Be prepared to help yourself.

In this modern age where everything can be accessed at the simple click of a button, too many people make the mistake of overlooking the importance of personal development. This is especially relevant when it comes to knowing your numbers and ratios, as to really get to grips with the 'nuts and bolts' of your margins, you need to be able to understand them.

It's a great idea to put a few hours aside each week to learn about and properly understand your numbers and figures. By all means, if this is not your strong point, then get a professional in to help you but you should still take the time and effort to learn as much as you can. Super-successful business owners don't leave it to chance; they make sure they know enough about everything in their business so no-one can take advantage of them. Invest the time in learning about it all.

Referral Master Nugget:

"Success does not depend so much on external help as on self-reliance."

Abraham Lincoln

Referral Master Tip # 58: It's all about confidence!

Don't be afraid of your numbers; let them inspire you, even if they are not what you thought they were.

As a business owner, it's so easy to fall into the trap of thinking you are doing better than you are. In the past, you may have been fearful about knowing the exact amount you're spending and earning. Don't be!

You can only improve when you know what you need to improve on.

If your car was low on fuel, would you continue to drive it at the risk of burning out? Of course you wouldn't; and the same concept applies to your business.

Be confident about your business. Take the courage to find out what is not working and use your wisdom to implement the changes your business needs in order to become successful.

Referral Master Nugget:

Your business is relying on you to take care of it, so make sure you know what it needs to survive.

Referral Master Tip # 59: Invest in good data.

In order to diligently keep track of your numbers and ratios, it's a good idea to invest in good data lists, if you can.

When purchasing data lists make sure that you:

- Do your research on the company you're buying from beforehand;
- Purchase lists that are relevant to your business only;
- Buy a small list as a trial before spending large amounts of money as most lists sold don't deliver what they promise.

Buying other people's lists should be seen as a last resort. Ideally, building your own list through marketing and reciprocal arrangements where others mail their list on your behalf will deliver much better results.

Referral Master Nugget:

"Quality is never an accident; it is always the result of high intention, sincere effort, intelligent direction and skilful execution; it represents the wise choice of many alternatives."

William A Foster

Referral Master Tip # 60: Stay on track!

Knowing your numbers thoroughly requires you to measure everything you do. Tracking Numbers is a great and effective tool for this.

These special telephone numbers can be set to divert to a number of your choice (i.e. your switchboard, mobile or call answering service) and give you an in-depth analysis of where your leads are coming from and what's working for you in terms of your marketing spend.

So, if 100 quality phone calls a month are coming from your A5 leaflet and only two quality phone calls are coming from your website, then you know where your money should be invested going forward (and you need to speak to your web developer as well!).

For a very low monthly cost, I use www.invoco.co.uk who are a great supply partner for us.

Referral Master Nugget:

Tracking Numbers will be the best small investment you make this year in your business.

Referral Master Tip # 61: Get to grips with online marketing

Whether you are website-savvy or a technophobe, the internet is here to stay! Internet marketing is an extremely influential and powerful tool and if you are serious about making a success of your business, you have to jump on board this ever-evolving culture.

If you are not confident in taking on any of this yourself, then learn from the best. Nigel Botterill's Entrepreneur's Circle is a great place to start and you can often get a trial membership at **www.e-cguru.co.uk** for just a few pounds a month.

Pay-per-click advertising is a good system to learn if you want to really get your teeth into internet marketing. Online social media engagement is also a fantastic place to build rapport.

Referral Master Nugget:

"Think big and don't listen to people who tell you it can't be done. Life's too short to think small."

Tim Ferriss

Referral Master Tip # 62: Don't waste your time on blind promotion!

When you set up a business, you automatically think that everyone is going to fall in love with this fantastic product or service you have created. While this kind of enthusiasm and optimism is admirable, you need to think realistically about *who* will benefit from your business.

If, for example, you send out a thousand leaflets or email a thousand companies, how will you know which sectors are creating the sales if you don't target effectively? Even more importantly, how will you know which people you are wasting your money and time on?

As much as you are head over heels in love with your product or service, and as much as you believe in it, you have to accept that it will be more attractive to certain groups of people than others.

Referral Master Nugget:

Invest your money wisely; invest it in the people who are likely to make you a decent profit. Otherwise, it's not an investment at all.

Referral Master Tip # 63: Get your name out there...

You may have the best product or service that has ever been invented; your business may have more potential than any other in its sector and you may be the most skilful person in your craft. But...if you don't show what you are made of, then no one will ever come knocking on your door (with a bag full of cash).

Contrary to popular belief, people still like to do business with people; people still prefer to communicate face-to-face than over the telephone or internet (especially when it comes to parting with money!).

Joining the right networking group can bring you referrals and contacts that greatly exceed your expectations. Successful networking, however, requires practice and it shouldn't be considered as a 'get-rich-quick or a quick-way to-sales scheme'.

Referral Master Nugget:

Networking requires you to put in the effort; it's not meant as an excuse to get out the office. That's why it's called net*working*, not net*sitting*, net*eating* or net*chatting!*

Referral Master Tip # 64: Put out!

There is absolutely no point in attending a networking group if you are going to sit in the corner and look on!

Walk around, smile, and appear confident and approachable. When the opportunity arises, try striking up a conversation by asking what the person does for a living and making them feel like you are genuinely interested in what they have to say. Ask questions such as, "How long have you been in business?" and "Do you mind if a take one of your business cards?"

Take the conversation slowly and listen to what the other person is saying. As soon as the person thinks that you are interested in their business, they will automatically show an interest in yours.

Once the connection has been established, then you can slowly introduce your company. Try not to come across as 'over pushy' as this will automatically put the other person off.

Referral Master Nugget:

"Sales are contingent upon the attitude of the salesman - not just the attitude of the prospect."

W. Clement Stone

Referral Master Tip # 65: Follow me!

Here are my top tips on being a successful networker:

- Smile;
- Be approachable;
- Carry business cards;
- Talk, don't sell;
- Ask questions...lots of them;
- Be confident;
- Dress smartly;
- Ask for contact details;
- Try different groups to find one that's right for you;
- Very Important - listen much, much more than you talk;

Referral Master Nugget:

Whenever you are going to a networking event, have a plan of what you want to achieve out of the event.

Building Your Keep-In-Touch Plan

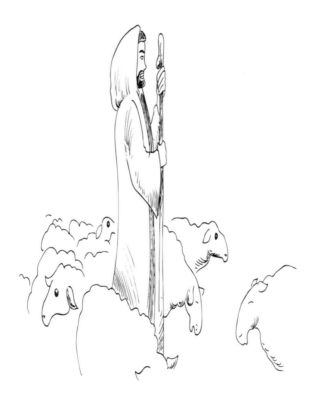

Referral Master Tip # 66: Be a farmer, not a hunter.

Don't worry, I am not talking about digging out your old and mucky wellingtons and heading to your nearest farm and tending to the local sheep! What I am saying is that you should nurture your relationships with clients instead of going 'in for the kill' for a one-off deal.

Your clients are your livelihood, your business and ultimately, your wages. That is why if you want to be successful and if you want to *continue* to be successful, you need to make the effort to build and maintain strong working relationships.

Referral Master Nugget:

Why waste time and money on expensive 'throwing mud at the wall' advertising in the hope that some will stick? If you build up a solid network of positive relationships with your contacts, then you will no longer need to 'cold call'. Over anything else, people buy from people they know, like and trust, so make it your priority to become that person.

Referral Master Tip # 67: Be who the others are not prepared to be!

Did you know that 80% of all businesses are either struggling or 'just getting by'? Did you also know that out of the 20% who are doing well, only 1% of these are super-successful? Why is this?

Because 80% of businesses are not prepared to go that extra mile; to do the things that others aren't doing.

In order for your business to propel ahead of your competitors, you need to consistently make an effort to be the best; to be the person your customers want you to be and to constantly keep on top of your game.

Treat your customers better than any of your competitors do and you'll be on the right track to getting in that 1%.

Referral Master Nugget:

"It is not the employer who pays the wages. Employers only handle the money. It is the customer who pays the wages...don't ever, ever forget that."

Henry Ford

Referral Master Tip # 68: Know your audience...

Knowing what makes your contacts 'tick', so to speak, will enable you to mould your communication in accordance with their personality. As a result, your approach will stand out from the majority of business who do not know how to or can't be bothered to incorporate these niceties.

Of course, I don't expect you to know the favourite colour or the favourite song of each of your contacts, but as your professional relationships develop, you should make it your concern to get a 'feel' for each of your contacts' personalities.

If, for example, you are speaking with your printer and they happen to mention that they are a soccer fan, make a note of it and ensure you update the details into your database, so that next time, you can incorporate a soccer-led approach into your communication.

Referral Master Nugget:

A good reputation is as powerful as a money- making machine, so make sure you show your contacts your best side.

Referral Master Tip # 69: Segment your audience!

The more contacts you have, then the more difficult it gets to know each of them on a personal level. Obviously, it isn't practical for anyone to expect you to know the likes and dislikes of thousands of contacts (phew!), but there are ways in which you can segment your contacts in order to make your communication more personable.

Gender is a great place to start when looking at ways at segmenting your audience. If you are a hairdresser, for example, then you would send out different promotional material to ladies as you would to gents.

Location is another easy way of separating your contacts. If a contact lives in America, then you would speak to them about different occurrences than you would to someone who lives in Scotland!

Business Type is also an effective way of targeting your approach. Your contacts down at the haulage company will probably not have the same interests as your accountant.

Referral Master Nugget:

There will always be exceptions to the rules but segmentation enables you to communicate on a more personal level without having to know your contacts 'inside and out'.

Referral Master Tip # 70: It's all about them...

It's a fact; the more you do for someone, the more they will do for you. Look at it from your own point of view; would you be more inclined to buy a product from someone who takes a general interest in your wellbeing and keeps in touch regularly, or from someone who you only ever hear from when they want something?

Remember that to make it all about you; you must firstly make it all about them.

The number one rule to being a master of this skill is to make the *real* reason you're communicating seem second priority. Put your contact's needs ahead of your own so that they feel they are being treated as a friend rather than a prospective client.

Referral Master Nugget:

"I forgot to shake hands and be friendly. It was an important lesson...."

Lee Lacocca

Referral Master Tip # 71: SPECIAL GUEST TIP:

Touch your customers - not like that!

Name: Richard Markie

Company: Blue Star Print Solutions

Website: www.bluestarprintsolutions.co.uk

"Having a varied and mixed method of 'touching' your customers is imperative in building reliable and strong relationships with them. Don't just use email to keep in touch with them – why not mix your method of communication by sending out some of the following:
• A Printed, regular Newsletter;
• Postcards on your customers Birthday offering them something or as a thank you card;
• Information emails to establish you as the expert in your field;
• Direct Mail – used correctly and <u>*personalised*</u>
• Offers relevant to their purchasing habits (this one could be email or sales letter);
• It can be through SMS marketing as well – keep your customers informed at each stage of your process.

Make sure your market is defined and a suitable message is created and finally, think of how it will be delivered you may have to change it to suit. Market, Message, Media."

Referral Master Tip # 72: Stand out from the crowd.

As you are reading this, hundreds of new businesses may be emerging from the minds of like-minded entrepreneurs. The industry is fast-paced and competitive, so you need to ensure that your business is the one that always stands out from the crowd.

When nurturing your professional relationships and creating your all-important 'keep in touch' plan, try to think of original, innovative ways to keep your contacts interested.

Special offers are always an effective way of attracting interest, and even though we are used to seeing 'deals' wherever we go, have you ever come across a product offering 17% or 13% off?

People have become too used to seeing round numbers such as 20% or 50% off, and familiarity does not turn heads! Be creative, be different and although they may be made up numbers, there is certainly no harm in testing a 21%, 17% or even a 13% off deal on a particular offer or service.

Referral Master Nugget:

Make your business the talking point amongst your contacts.

Referral Master Tip # 73: Do the hard things to make selling easy!

For a good business person, selling should never be difficult. Good business people put in all the hard work *beforehand*, so that closing a sale is easy.

Unsuccessful business owners, however, are the ones that can never be bothered or don't know how to put in the effort of nurturing those money-making relationships.

If you want a prosperous business, you have to consistently work hard at your professional relationships.

A great example of this came from a local car repair business that (before the bad winter weather set in) ordered a supply of branded car windscreen ice scrapers, and planned ahead by writing a sales letter. The repair team got out early when snow fell in their local town and attached the scrapers, with their letter (containing an MOT offer) to windscreens. What a great idea!

Referral Master Nugget:

Do the hard things that others can't or won't do to make the selling easy for you.

Referral Master Tip # 74: Mind over matter.

In business, many people use the profiling principle to segment people's personalities (and yes, people are usually a mix of each to some varying degree or another). This is of course optional to you. You can certainly use DISC, Belbin and other personality tools available.

This skill will enable you to better understand your customers, clients, staff and suppliers.

For more information on personality profiling check out;

- Wikipedia – personality profiling
- DISC Profiling
- Tim Templeton - Business through relationship style in four types

Referral Master Nugget:

Understanding different personality traits and what makes people tick is how smart businesses can build rapport, and create compelling marketing messages and customer offers that engage with more prospect customers than their competitors.

Referral Master Tip # 75: SPECIAL GUEST TIP:

Be smart and use your Smartphone!

Name: David Standing

Company: mymobweb.com

Website: www.mymobweb.com

"Did you know that over 40% of emails are now opened on Smartphones? Indeed, depending on your target audience that figure can be as high as 80%! And in most instances this is the only device that emails are opened on. That means that the recipient will simply delete the copy of the email, which is sitting on their desktop computer. So if you want the recipients to respond via a website, don't forget to include a link to a page that is optimised for Smartphones. If that sounds complicated – don't worry it isn't! You can use a variety of systems to create a mobile version of your website sales or customer sign- up page or ask your web designer to do it for you."

Referral Master Tip # 76: No complacency!

Complacency is one of the greatest reasons why many businesses do not reach their full potential. It's easy to let a certain amount of success tame the hunger you had at the beginning. The example below demonstrates how complacency can have an effect on your business:

Sue has owned a hairdressing salon for the past five years. At first, Sue worked tirelessly to ensure that her salon would become the most successful in her area. Keen to set herself apart, Sue offered innovative hairstyles at reasonable prices, kept her key contacts up to date of current promotions and liaised regularly with her suppliers. Inevitably, it wasn't long before valuable referrals were being made and the business was flourishing.

Content with her current level of success, Sue became complacent. Sue felt that she no longer had to 'sell' her services. What she didn't know, however, is that her contacts were becoming increasingly aware of the change in communication. No longer regularly keeping in touch with her contacts, Sue's competitors' services had caught up and were starting to outshine hers.

Referral Master Nugget:

Never assume that you are in the position to 'kick back' and unwind. Be mindful of businesses who could overtake you and steal your customers.

Referral Master Tip # 77: Fail to plan, plan to fail...

When you consider what happened to our salon owner in the previous example, it is clear that this business owner did not make sufficient and durable plans to ensure that her business maintained the level of success it experienced at the beginning.

When nurturing your professional relationships, it is crucial that you understand that this is an ongoing venture; not something you merely do just to secure a sale. Your business is only ever as successful as yesterday's profits, so always make sure you plan ahead.

So, I recommend that you map out your initial thoughts into the start of a time-based programme where you begin to segment your ideas into themes and work out what you plan to do for the different levels within your database.

Referral Master Nugget:

Without a plan you will have a roadmap to nowhere and any road can take you there...it's just not where you need to be, to be super-successful.

Referral Master Tip # 78: Impress!

As always, when looking at ways in which you can nurture your professional relationships and create an impressive 'keep in touch' plan, you should try to appeal to your customers' specific tastes.

If you have a group of contacts that are specifically interested in art, for instance, then a creative event may be more attractive than a sporting event. Remember that these actions are meant to 'treat' your contacts and help build relationships, so tailor the decisions around them and not you. A meal out before or after the event can work as well as expensive hospitality in the venue, so these events don't need to cost a fortune.

Referral Master Nugget:

It's all about them, not about you, so make sure you create interesting and engaging ways to interact that meet your contacts' needs and not just your own.

Referral Master Tip # 79: You are your business!

As a business owner, you represent your company, its values and its success. When building your 'keep in touch' plan, only plan to do the things that you are certain you are able to do. If, for example, you are terrified of heights, don't plan a breakfast meeting at the top of revolving restaurant! Similarly, if you can't afford to do something; don't plan to do it but make sure you add it to your goals and aim to be in a position to do it next month, quarter or year.

Your 'keep in touch' plan should always be realistic and something that is a true reflection of who you are. Remember that your contacts should always see your best side, so don't risk doing something that shows you at your worst!

Referral Master Nugget:

You don't have to be rolling in cash to show your contacts that you care. In an industry where 80% of people will not be doing what you are doing, small gestures can make a big impact.

Referral Master Tip # 80: RANDOM ACTS OF KINDNESS (RAOKs)

ROAK's are subtle actions carried out to get your profile out into the community. This technique is all about 'making someone's day'.

You could consider incorporating actions such as leaving some change at the vending machine or paying a stranger's toll. It's all about surprising someone with a thoughtful act. Of course, you are a business person and you would leave a RAOKMan style postcard or business card that's beneficial to your business. Again, it's all about setting your business apart.

Referral Master Nugget:

Each month, I buy a new business book and get four copies - one for our own business library for staff, the other three I send to one of my key referral partners with a RAOK message.

Join in the RAOKMan fun at www.facebook.com/RAOKMan

Referral Master Tip # 81: Communication is everything!

How often do you hear from your accountant, your landlord or your office cleaning contractors?

Probably only when they want something!

Try to get into the habit of thinking about your contacts; if you know they have an important event coming up, make a note of it so you can ask them how it went when the time comes. Similarly, if you hear about something going on within their local community or to do with their business sector, strike up a conversation focusing around this subject.

Whilst there is the advantage these days of email and social media, for regular communication, a 'just keeping in touch' phone call wins hands down.

Referral Master Nugget:

Communicating with your contacts and showing them that you are thinking of them even when there is nothing in it for you will go a long way in developing your relationships.

Committing to the Plan and
Goal Setting

Referral Master Tip # 82: The habit of a lifetime!

It is always difficult to commit to something; but think of the things we are already committed to without realising:

Eating, drinking, socialising, using the internet, texting, talking, sleeping... the list goes on and on.

Now, you may not think these things require a lot of 'commitment' but in reality, they do. As a child, getting into the 'habit' of sleeping through the night would have been difficult, but now, you do it automatically without thinking. Now, as an adult, it has become embedded into your routine as something that is essential to your survival. Try to apply this notion to your business and try to remember that there are some essential habits that must be formed in order for your business to survive and thrive!

Referral Master Nugget:

"We must first make our habits, and then our habits make us."

John Dryden

Referral Master Tip # 83: Make your mind on the money!

If you want to be a millionaire, you have to act like a millionaire and live like a millionaire. Now, I am certainly not recommending that you go and purchase a million pounds worth of flash cars on multiple credit cards (please don't do that)! What I *am* saying is that you should start to get into the mindset of thinking rich- even when you are broke!

Super-successful people have always had a vision of the kind of life they've wanted to lead; in their minds, they have seen themselves living in riches and have implemented their plans to ensure that vision became reality!

Referral Master Nugget:

"I've never been poor, only broke. Being poor is a frame of mind. Being broke is only a temporary situation."

Mike Todd

Referral Master Tip # 84: You can do it!

It Couldn't Be Done

Edgar Albert Guest

Somebody said that it couldn't be done,
But, he with a chuckle replied
That "maybe it couldn't," but he would be one
Who wouldn't say so till he'd tried.
So he buckled right in with the trace of a grin
On his face. If he worried he hid it.
He started to sing as he tackled the thing
That couldn't be done, and he did it.

Somebody scoffed: "Oh, you'll never do that;
At least no one has done it";
But he took off his coat and he took off his hat,
And the first thing we knew he'd begun it.
With a lift of his chin and a bit of a grin,
Without any doubting or quiddit,
He started to sing as he tackled the thing
That couldn't be done, and he did it.

There are thousands to tell you it cannot be done,
There are thousands to prophesy failure;
There are thousands to point out to you one by one,
The dangers that wait to assail you.
But just buckle it in with a bit of a grin,
Just take off your coat and go to it;
Just start to sing as you tackle the thing
That "couldn't be done," and you'll do it.

Referral Master Tip # 85: Think big to be big!

Everyone wants to be successful; you want to be successful (otherwise you would be a reading a novel instead of this book), and now, after discovering the secrets of referrals, you should have a good idea of what you need to do in order to make it happen.

Now, it's time to start implementing everything you've learned and make a commitment to seeing it through to the end. This is the part where 80% of businesses fail.

Super-successful business owners set, write down, and review their goals regularly. They make a commitment to themselves to take MASSIVE action to implement what they set out for themselves, their families and their businesses. They make achievement of short, medium and long-term goals part of their daily routine.

Referral Master Nugget:

Learning how to do something is easy; actually doing it is the difficult part. Don't' be one of the 80% of business owners who can't be bothered; be one of the few who do, to help you become super-successful.

Referral Master Tip # 86: The lifestyle of a successful business owner...

I would recommend, that every day (and throughout the day when the pressure seems too much), you remind yourself of what success means to you. Think about the kind of lifestyle you want and visualise yourself living it. Maybe you see yourself living in a tropical country or maybe you want to be able to buy a bigger house for you and your family. Whatever your motivation for success, keep it with you at all times.

Would a rugby player endure a gruelling and painful game if he thought there was no chance of winning? Of course not!

Remember that the whole point of hard work is to achieve something at the end of it; and as long as you don't lose your vision of what you want, you will work as hard as is necessary.

Referral Master Nugget:

Create a vision board of the things you wish to achieve - be it a car, a new home, or a luxury holiday. It's amazing what you can achieve when you have a vision of where you want to get to. Pinterest is a good on-line tool for this.

Referral Master Tip # 87: Break it down...

Having to commit yourself to a goal for the rest of your working life can seem somewhat daunting. That is why I recommend that you create a daily, weekly, monthly, and yearly plan. That way, you are able to work from goal to goal.

Every evening, plan what you must do the next day and at the end of each week, plan for your following week and so on. It may sound regimented and you may not be used to working to such a firm schedule, but you will be surprised at how much more you will get done once you actually know what you are meant to be doing!

Think about it this way; would you travel to a holiday destination without packing a suitcase? Of course not!

Referral Master Nugget:

"Unless commitment is made, there are only promises and hopes; but no plans."

Peter F. Drucker

Referral Master Tip # 88: Subconscious planning...

Do you plan to brush your teeth tomorrow morning?

Do you plan to sleep tonight?

Of course, the answer is 'yes'. Why am I asking you this?

Because these are plans that you subconsciously make that allow your life to function on a day-to-day basis; they are integrated so deeply into your mind, that you do not even give them a second thought. It is said that if you do something for 21 days without missing a day then this will be embedded into your subconscious mind as an everyday occurrence and a habit will have been formed (good or bad). So we are looking to create a good habit here where you build a positive attitude towards your business plans and goals.

Referral Master Nugget:

Change something for the good...start a 21 day plan starting today and follow /action it for 21 consecutive days to make the change permanent.

Referral Master Tip # 89: Harvard knows best!

There is a much-quoted study from students of Harvard Business School. In the 1970s, Harvard undertook a study to find out how successful their 1950s past graduates had been and to ascertain what made the difference between those who were super-successful and those who were not. What they found is that 3% of those ex-students had built a personal wealth ten times that of the remaining 97% combined and when they analysed why, one of the key driving factors that came out was that all of the top 3% had, and continued to set clearly defined goals, regularly reviewed those goals, and had a focused implementation action plan to achieve them.

As you grow as a business person, and as your business develops, your goals will inevitably alter. The crucial thing is to keep your commitment.

Referral Master Nugget:

"You can't plough a field simply by turning it over in your mind."

Gordon B. Hinckley

Referral Master Tip # 90: Read all about it...

To help you set, track and achieve your goals, I recommend you take a look at:

- Jim Rohn's *One Year Success* programme

  www.jimrohn.com

- Brian Mayne's goal-mapping programme: *Visualising Goals* - www.liftinternational.com

- Darren Hardy's (Editor and Publisher of Success Magazine): *Design Your Best Year Ever* - *www.success.com*

- Chris Williams - *Goal Getting* www.goalgetting.co.uk

- Bernie de Souza's Goal Setting programme - www.berniedesouza.com

Referral Master Nugget:

Focused activity makes a massive difference on getting you to where you want to be.

Referral Master Tip # 91: You can be that person!

Many people are so afraid to fail that they don't even try to succeed. Out of all the business owners who are reading this book right now, only 20% will have the courage to put their learning into action. I guarantee that those 20% will be the ones driving the Ferrari, going on exotic holidays or buying that dream house.

MAKE SURE THAT YOU ARE THAT PERSON!

You have had the initiative to set up your own business; you have had the courage to start from scratch and you have the inspiration to make it a success.

You are made of the same substances as the most successful people on the planet, so have the confidence to believe that you can be whoever you want to be!

Referral Master Nugget:

"In order to succeed, your desire for success should be greater than your fear of failure."

Bill Cosby

Referral Master Tip # 92: A new you!

Don't let your actions of the past have a detrimental effect on your actions of the future. Maybe you have never been any good at making commitments; maybe you have always given up before you have even got started; and maybe you have always been the 'Master of Procrastination'! Who cares!?

Today is a new day and a chance to become the new you! Remember that mistakes form some of the best learning tools, and even though you may have fallen down in the past, you have always got back on your feet; otherwise you wouldn't be here, reading this today.

Allow your negative past experiences to be the reason they never happen again; not the reason you no longer try.

Referral Master Nugget:

"Be changed and the world around you begins to change."

Gerald Epstein

Summary

Relax, unwind and take a breather because as of this moment, you are now equipped with the tips that you need to get your business into the top 20% of businesses! *Phew!*

Now, we don't expect you to remember every single thing we have just covered (you will need to recap and review in your own time), but to make sure you start implementing this new knowledge straight away (we'll let you have a cup of tea first), we have re-capped on the most important tips that you should carry out over the next day, week and month.

Remember that this is just a starting point and you will need to consistently put in the effort for these tips to work. **This book will not work if it remains sat on your bookshelf!**

So, grab that cuppa and then get cracking!

Referral Master Tip # 93: Stop, look, listen!

Before you do anything else, remember what we said earlier; there is a common denominator that merges the unsuccessful; failure to listen!

Even if you have the strongest of visions, you must always be prepared to listen to the experts who know the industry or market place inside out!

As you travel along your journey to being super-successful, you will always need advice. Even when you have 'made it' and you are sitting on your paradise island looking at the new Ferrari brochure, you will still need advice. Success is an ongoing venture; something that requires maintenance and preservation, so never underestimate the importance of continued learning and listening!

Referral Master Nugget:

"Courage is what it takes to stand up and speak; courage is also what it takes to sit down and listen."

Winston Churchill

Referral Master Tip # 94: Be the optimist!

The mind is an incredible powerful tool, and if you think positively, you'll live positively. Remember that you are your business, and the only thing stopping you from achieving your gaols is you.

If you make the ongoing effort to be the optimist, you will soon start to realise that there are opportunities everywhere. The secret is that only optimistic eyes will see them.

Start by trying to get into the habit of looking for the positive in everything you do. Even when you have a bad day (which you will get), you have to keep going, and remember why you are doing what you are doing.

Referral Master Nugget:

"Write it on your heart that every day is the best day in the year."

Ralph Waldo Emerson

Referral Master Tip # 95: Be someone they remember!

As reiterated throughout this book, reputation sells, so you must make sure you make that great first impression from day one! A good way to ensure that you give your business the reputation it deserves is to start thinking from the perspective of your customers and referral partners.

Think about how you would feel if you were introduced to your business. Would you be left with a long lasting impression or would your message merge with the thousands of others in your sector? What would make your business stand out?

Referral Master Nugget:

Good impressions count... but bad impressions last a whole lot longer in people's minds.

Referral Master Tip # 96: Make decisions and take action!

In between a pipedream and a pipeline for success sits implemented goals and actions, so make sure you make the effort to do the things that will turn your dreams into reality.

Making a decision is easy; people make decisions everyday, but how many of these people actually put them into action? Only successful people.

Procrastination is one of the biggest traits of the un-wealthy so don't put off until tomorrow what you can do today!

Remember that dreams may see skyscrapers, but only implemented plans and actions will be the foundation that builds them.

Referral Master Nugget:

"If you don't know exactly where you're going, how will you know when you get there?"

Steve Maraboli

Referral Master Tip # 97: Get a new best friend!

Now that you are fully committed to building a super-successful business, it's time you said 'hello' to your new best friend - your database!

Remember that your new and transformed database will be the kindest and most generous friend you've ever known - if you treat it well! It's all about give and take with your database, and if you want to take, you must be prepared to give. If you nurture your database, communicate through it, and give it the information it needs to function, then you will prosper from the opportunities it creates for you; it's simple.

Referral Master Nugget:

Remember to build the biggest asset your business will ever own with care, attention and sound planning...your database will then bring you a world of business opportunities in return.

Referral Master Tip # 98: Make the most of the internet!

Whether you like it or not, the internet is here to stay and is one of the most powerful networking tools around. Social networking sites such as Facebook and LinkedIn can provide massive platforms to build your referral sphere, and can be highly advantageous to your business.

Remember to think about how your social network contacts may be of benefit to your referral plan. Look at the Facebook friends who are in similar sectors as you and think about what you can gain from the connection. Think about the chain of referrals these contacts could bring.

Referral Master Nugget:

Social contacts have jobs and contacts that can open up two-way opportunities as much as business contacts...you just need to do some research and talk to them.

Referral Master Tip # 99: Remember the power of four!

A database works best when it is arranged and segmented in accordance to your priority of contacts.

If you allow yourself the time to get to grips with your VIRPs, Golds, Silvers and Developing contacts, you will soon be on your way to creating a highly advantageous database!

Here's a quick reminder of those all-important segments:

VIRPs- very important referral partners

Golds- the next 20-30 influential contacts

Silvers- the contacts you are in the process of building a relationship with

Developing- the contacts you hope to develop a relationship with.

Referral Master Nugget:

Remember that the level of communication that you have with your contacts from each segment will differ, so be diligent during the segmenting process.

Referral Master Tip # 100: Give to get!

As an up and coming super-successful business owner, you can never allow yourself to think that you can get anything for nothing.

Remember to think about the relationships you have built in your life so far and think about how different they are now to when they begun. Think of the ways you have nurtured these relationships, and try to get into the habit of applying this concept to your professional contacts.

Don't forget that all relationships (be they professional or personal) must work on a two-way street and that you can't expect to get anything without giving something first.

Referral Master Nugget:

"First you must sow to be able to reap your harvest in your Autumn years."

Jim Rohn

Referral Master Tip #: 101... GET YOUR HANDS ON AN EXCLUSIVE COPY OF THE CUSTOMER PIPELINE FOR A LIFETIME TOOLKIT!

If you've found this book helpful, then you will greatly benefit from the Customer Pipeline for a Lifetime Toolkit. Jam-packed with everything you will ever need to become a Referral Master, this widely acclaimed toolkit will drive your business to greater profitability without the need for expensive cold calling and 'throwing mud at the wall' advertising!

Referral Master Nugget:

If you are serious about becoming a super-successful business owner, then make the best investment you will ever make and grab your copy today at www.referralmaster.info

Congratulations in advance on your new, profitable, thriving, and booming business!

CUSTOMER PIPELINE
FOR A LIFETIME

Toolkit Offer for 101 Hints and Tips Readers

www.referralmaster.info

Dreams Don't Open Doors, People Do!

In a recent International survey, 97% of business owners stated that they rely on word of mouth/referral marketing to grow their business, but only 3% of businesses actually have a plan to achieve this.

So, for the remaining 94% of businesses who don't have a plan yet, we are here to help you every step of the way with the Customer Pipeline for a Lifetime referral development system.

Take a look at the Customer Pipeline for a Lifetime product at http://delivr.com/2nyqv for the special reduced price on both the on-line and the Premium Deluxe versions of the toolkit.

http://delivr.com/2nyqv

119

www.referralmaster.co.uk